# Blindsight

# Blindsight

poems by

Carol Vanderveer Hamilton

Carnegie Mellon University Press

Pittsburgh 2005

ACKNOWLEDGMENTS

Acknowledgment is gratefully made to the following periodicals:

CEILIDH (chapbook series): Newport, 1900; Alptrauma; Xenophilia; Haunted; Sleepwalkers; Sad; Toward the End; The Glass Children; Applesauce; Nursery Rhymes; Metanarrative

THE CIMARRON REVIEW: Arctic; Loss; Residue

THE CUMBERLAND POETRY REVIEW: Costume Drama; Buzz; The Other Loneliness

FIVE A.M.: Blind Spot; Film Noir

FRANK: A Revelation

KESTREL: The Delicate World; Unter den Linden

THE NORTH AMERICAN REVIEW: Aesthetics and Politics

THE PARIS REVIEW: Narcolepsy; Delirium; Night Thoughts; May Day

THE PITTSBURGH POST-GAZETTE: In the Second Degree

POETRY MISCELLANY: Refuge

SALMAGUNDI: Fugitives; Revolution

SOCIAL ANARCHISM: New World Order; Happenstance; Daylight

The publication of this book is supported by a grant from the Pennsylvania Council on the Arts.

PENNSYLVANIA COUNCIL ON THE ARTS

Library of Congress Control Number: 2004100915
ISBN 0-88748-432-8

Printed and bound in the United States of America

10 9 8 7 6 5 4 3 2 1

## Contents

## I. Scotoma



## II. Double Vision

## III. Hyperopia

*Enable with perpetual light*
*The dulness of our blinded sight.*

The Book of Common Prayer

# I.

# Scotoma

*Who are you?*
*Mine eyes are not o' th' best; I'll tell you straight.*
Lear, V. iii

## Blindsight

My eye wanders across radiators and stuffed toys
seeking a point of rest
in the floorboards, where invisible
meteors enter. Nobody warned us

about the dangers of this country:
hailstorms, shuddering volcanoes,
black firs burnished like bayonets.

Like fallen angels,
we run through blindness.

An ordinary day of extraordinary clouds:
swallows soar over suspension bridges,
fractures flaw the fastidious light,
windows transmit signals.

Having spent hours polishing the lenses
of my sunglasses, hoping that a truth
would insinuate itself
through them, I looked toward the sea,

ascended a hypotenuse into sleep
so that later, in fact, now
in the resumption of ordinariness, I hear
ink sinking through linen paper,

the cries of abandoned animals,
yesterday's F minor chord.

From its retreat the dawn returns,
and in the fog the waves unfold:

a childhood wish no child remembers.

## Arctic

*The invisible spheres were formed in fright.*
— Melville

Darkness elides all distinctions:
beauty and rank, color and age,

advancing like a colonizing nation
through the wounds and fissures of daylight

until occupation has that cold, clear character
so admired by explorers of the North

when, in a fever, they gazed on the ice
and hallucinated distant cities

blazing above their rivers,
the Thames, the Seine, the Rhine.

Soothed by the shortwave radio,
they dreamed of improbable rescues

until darkness and cold made a meal of them,
expelling their bodies at dawn.

Then there was nothing to hear except
avalanches and random explosions

offshore, in the visible world they had
left behind for good.

## Newport, 1900

He was twenty, blond, doomed. It was only
yesterday that he entered the French windows,

wincing at us as we sipped our sherry,
turning the pages of travel books, pretending

not to hear. His hands shaking,
he broke everything he touched.

"Merry Christmas," he said, not smiling. I looked
past him at the huntboard, where silver

gleamed among folded shadows,
the house with its recesses, unopened

rooms. He clattered upstairs.
In an open blue doorway we saw strangers

bearing umbrellas, soaked
in the afternoon glare. Sure enough,

in the morning he was gone,
having stolen a shotgun, croquet mallet,

teddy bear. The glint of his hair
lingered. *I will never*

*forgive or remember,* the note read,
so we sat on the patio with our drinks

and watched the glittering water,
its sharks' teeth and memorabilia.

## Refuge

I'm mesmerized by the differences

between several stray bits of air:  the heft
of some chunks, the relative lightness of others,

how light adheres to make subtle colors
as I peel the air off my eyes.  Some people

think that these differences are glaring
because of the way sunlight and dark slicing through

leave traces of blood, a square root sign, or a sickle.
But I find it hard to describe a piece of air,

except when our bodies get in the way
and we can see ourselves far off

and haunted, the dead
ready to ambush us in our sleep.

I need to hole up for a while.  Not in Montana
or Chenonceau, but in some country

where my shadow would cast its own shadow
across water that would mysteriously disappear.

A motel somewhere, its apostrophe
out of order.  The desert beginning to sear

in the midnight sun.  A man on the phone

cries weakly for air, as if trapped underwater
a hundred leagues from the surface of the sky,

someone profound and damaged, whose face
absorbs more light as it fades,

And maybe I should answer him.  Say,
*Yes. Okay. I guess that's true,*

before he begins to scream.

## Arles

The painting was blue and yellow.
A landscape, it screamed
of a blind sky averting its face

from blind figures staring up at it
for solace or recognition.
In this vast world, we shrink with loneliness

sleep with blankets over our faces,
hearing the heart beat, like a clock.
Outside there are fields falling

over cliffs, into abysses; waves
breaking smoothly, with foamy flourishes;
the rain, monotonous and persistent,

like a rejected lover, stalking us.

Gnarled, the apple trees; secretive, the olive grove;
painfully brilliant & manic, the sunflowers.

Occasionally, a human figure—
diminished, fugitive— with a sickle
walks into the horizon toward

the vanishing point,
the locus of all mathematics,
where zero times zero equals

all the nothing there is.

## Metanarrative

In which we are woken abruptly from our dreams,
bundled into carriages and driven

across snowblind landscapes to a strange city.
The story falters here. We are separated.

Denounced, locked in cells, forgotten.
The snow ages outside the bars,

developing creases and folds, and the thin sky
becomes, alternately, a mirror and a lens

reminding me of you and you of me. Then
years or days later, when they let me out,

I saunter into the sunlight,
vexed and happy at once, for there is

no end to this story and no story
to this story; the rest are gone,

and the reticent brain retreats under its awnings
to imagine something else:

a dolphin-philosopher
pondering ruined Atlantis, while the sea

rolls on, feigning innocence.

## Sad

I am sad, Horatio.

I am not as I once was, as I
imagined myself to be, moving
deliberately under Spanish moss

while Cadillacs foundered in swamps.

The dead glided past me, gracefully reticent,
goodbye or what served as goodbye
as we glanced at each other

like estranged and remorseful lovers.

And who would imagine I'd
see my childhood again, ripe fruit bursting,
everywhere I'd slept?

Thunderstorms beheaded the jonquils

till the grass, florid, incommensurate,
slid beneath my feet into snow or what
screamed like snow, and I was

incommunicado in some smash of light.

## Applesauce

In our heyday the winesaps flourished,

the sky came when we called it,
and dusk drank the crabgrass in every backyard.
Now we are both sorry we did what we did:

having fallen, slipped out of bounds
as our skateboards went out of control,
punching perfect holes in the air.

When autumn came down by the river,
the sidewalks shed broadsides of discarded light,
and dead leaves blew in like aerograms,

announced we were sorry we'd lived as we'd lived:
our solitary bedrooms, the weight of our wrists,
the turntable spinning silently.

Squinting at the mirror, I could see the bruise
where a football had crashed my eyesocket; he was
sorry, real sorry, he did what he did.

The fences I'll climb over
are no impediment to memory; my eye waters,
galaxies blear, at last the orchard

where apple trees spread their fragrance.
All possibility of change
is arrested, because dead starlight

will sail past me forever, leaving
a dull sheen on the grass
when I close my eyes.

## The Other Loneliness

The angle of trees against the windows:
nothing can pull you farther than the light.
Already the horizon is leaving without you.

Again the quicksilver shadows of birds
flying across long waters to the north.
They began a journey long ago

and are still yearning for its sweetness
to overcome them, a density of movement
taking them beyond the last shoreline

to the place the heart breaks cleanly
and boats drift without passengers
under a sky that does not alter its repose.

## Loss

In gasps and shudders of light,
as great pools of water form in the distance,
certain delirious dreams dissolve,

leaving their residue behind
at the back of the eyes and the corners of the mouth
where desire and sadness intersect

because loss shapes everything,

even what you seem to possess
most securely, as on Sunday afternoons
reading the *Times*, talking on the phone

long distance to a childhood friend,
for sometimes the heart-stopping beauty
of the visible world is veiled

by restrictions and routine,
and those dreams that cling to the lips
flake off like burned skin

while past and future seem equally remote,

as if life were no more than this *now* —
a mountaineer
plunging from a cliff.

## Alptrauma

Someone's abandoned car, someone's disciple,
he recalls porcelain figures clustered
on marble tables,
the house in Zermatt, miniature nights,

how storm windows rattled when he was a child:
migratory world
with strangers at the gate.

When the night makes a left at his door,
depositing sand on the threshold,
he carves his initials on desultory space

and flails in the sheets, describing
the trajectory of his absence:
he will orbit his body before he falls,

and the ocean,
a curved thought,
will never forget him.

He wonders if he'll wake up. His hands
cold, repudiating him,
catching the train to Tomsk: he doesn't

care, he doesn't need them anymore.

## Blind Spot

It has to do with the way
cats choose the most complex route
across the room, over bookshelves and stereo speakers,
circuitous, indirect, as if they do not want

to admit it: they come to be near you.

Sirius, the Dog Star,
drools his thin spittle of light
over the cracked, punctuated surfaces
of asphalt, plaster, and glass.

Junkyards glitter by the roadside.
Industrial wastelands pulsate in the heat.

The ancient Leica
with its still perfect lens can't capture this
imperfection; painters
can't represent it. The cat

sits at last on your shoulder, smiling

at having traduced all straight lines,
which are like the lies
humans tell each other: that order predominates,
that providence will rescue you

from yourself in the nick of time,
time nicked, damaged, stolen, jailed,
a blur in the blind spot
behind the rearview mirror

seconds before the crash.

## Rondeau

No one was invited to this dance,

this rondeau, with its perigrinations,
these swoops into motionlessness

when the sky and the world hold forth
like orators, and there is a visible grace

in the very idea of grace
as if large illuminated ominous shapes

gathered round in rows, raised their arms,
advanced gradually toward a damaged center,

dissipated and retreated, returned and solidified,
the way thoughts themselves move,

magnetic, obsessive, desultory,
until the music comes to a halt

and the instrumentalists put down their bows,
bow, and walk offstage, leaving us

forlorn on a foggy afternoon
as railroad tracks meet at infinity

and all the trains collide.

## Heat Lightning

The deer, having hidden all day among the pines,
emerge with the twilight, approaching

our strands of light among the hills.

We are quiet at last, and they are quiet as always,
moving along the borders of our sleep.

There must be a kind of peace
in that valley where night is afloat

so that if I walked there, my body
would move in an electrified calm.

But I am afraid I would meet the inverse of myself:
a stranger remote from all roads and lights,

wandering there, violent, among the night animals.

Heat lightning I understand.
The body's trapped warmth, the brain flaring

as if to release its pent-up existence
and fitful flashes of desire. The deer have moved

through that desire and stand on the other side
behind a membrane, breathing

that coolness they carry with them.
Their delicate bodies and movements

are an alphabet we can't decipher. I want
to live here, where the night animal world

borders ours, and we catch a glimpse
of that beauty so far away from us.

Like lightning, momentary: we can see in the dark.

## Night Thoughts

Darkness immigrates from the floorboards
into the headboard of the bed, where the skull
crunched against it, dreams flat dreams.

The breathing is even, like a chant.
There is something plangent about the bathroom light,
a cello solo, boring a neat hole

in the head, bonedust flying, the eye like soft cheese,
the hands raised once, then crumpling.
Even pressed together, we sleep alone.

Then there's nothing except this pain in the wrist
after the hand has flinched from the head,
and the sky has broken into blisters of light,

raw, painful, the coming to consciousness.
What moves toward you, uneven, menacing?
All that you have lost—

the detritus of nightmares,
those younger, cast-off selves, each sideways glance
of hatred or desire into

the mind's cold purpose
and the heart's unfathomable
ambivalence.

# II.
# Double Vision

LEAR: *Out of my sight!*

KENT: *See better, Lear, and let me still remain*
*The true blank of thine eye.*

Lear, I. i

## In the Second Degree

Sadness has its own laws, its regulations:
gestures of resignation, like lost coins
on the pavement, sparkle and spin.

Choked with tears, the heart, the voice.
Staring us in the face, an inveterate liar,
the world blinks repeatedly.

No one is listening.  Wind
or window: no distinction,
no eight-cylinder motor idling or

positive ions in the acorn soup.  Instead
this cacophony of silence,
deadbeat, deadpan— like Bogart

and the Eiffel Tower in one freeze frame,
everything tilted, an old fedora,
the rain streaming down sunglasses past

Duchamp's urinal into
Warhol's blood-stained wineglass.
Art, love, and sadness:

second-degree murder,
second-degree burns: please
take me home with you.

## Film Noir

"You're so *pisse-élégant*," she said, smiling,
at his lacquered face, his walnut eyes
reflecting candlelight (Strauß

in the distance) "with your Swiss banker's glasses
and your cool disdain for the poor
who sleep outside on heating vents.

You went to Yale, didn't you,
where you paid a scholarship boy to
take your exams; you drove a '65

Volvo P 1800 convertible
to the coast on weekends
for lobster and sex at your grandmother's cottage—"

"You know me too well," he said smoothly
(his voice was like cognac)
removing the chased silver derringer from his

greatcoat pocket. "This too
belonged to my grandmother" (waving it,
nuzzling her neck with it). His

body, when they found it, lay fallen with
one arm raised, as if
interrupted in the minuet.

*His net worth beyond*
*estimation,* the papers said, *why would he— ?*

She left, smiling vaguely, noting
imperfections of polish on the brass banisters,
the quality of sunlight

spilled across the flagstones, drenching
the solemn procedures of the dark:
often rehearsed, never memorized.

## Azimuth

Standing outside in the dark,
among the comets and asteroids, the snow

falling delicately upon balconies
like a discourse barely audible,

an astronomer stares through the telescope
on the rooftop, thinking

about stars and celestial debris,
how old the earth is and how far away

the closest galaxy,
and, almost as remote, the beloved,

who starlike traverses the distance, leaving
a trail of sparks on the void

a disintegrating script, whose syllables
the astronomer desperately

seeks to decipher
as if it could explain everything— passion,

history, the natural world—

and thereby cure him of this malaise,
these lunar bouts of longing.

## Unter den Linden

Her lover stands with an umbrella
at an ice-cream truck, reading

*Die Zeit,* dreaming at the
rough edges of his heart about her

flesh, her hands on his hips.
At a café, reading *Der Spiegel,*

sipping something cold and sweet,
she muses on him. There's an ardent

bruise on the inside of her
thigh. It's July. Swallows

sway in scintillas of light,
a unicyclist passes, arms in the air,

fat tourists photograph her as she flicks
past advertisements and disasters.

Twilight seeps like water
from the clouds, when they both

look up, catch sight of one another.
An exchange of gazes— fire and

shadow. Cobalt flag on a balcony.
The skinned world, its raw presence

momentarily, stingingly real.

## Buzz

### I.

The air is intolerable, like cheese gone bad
beer cans left open overnight, cigarette smoke
in a closed room of men playing poker.

It's Wednesday or March. Light
stains the teeth and enhances each flaw
in the worried visage. Everything

is almost something else, and nothing
matters more, or less, than this:
the stale silence between thoughts,

the vacancies between perceptions,
a world sunk in human detritus,
lulled by the ruthless buzz of traffic.

Meanwhile a college freshman listens to
Rachmaninoff's Second Symphony, weeping
into her pillow, vaguely longing

for a man's hands on her skin, a touch
both affectionate and keen. Allergies
plague her neighbor, an accountant

with blunt fingertips, whose idea of a good time
is to sleep it off. He'll sneeze
all afternoon as the sunlight filters

through plastic Venetian blinds,
spilling oddly beautiful patterns
on the cheap carpet.

II.

Unexpectedly, a rupture in the synapses,
an elision of thought. He speaks.
She questions. He retreats.

Oak trees burst into flame, but the phone rings
all night long. In a wink
weeks pass. Misunderstandings burst

into bloom. Lust persists.
A man in a convertible reads
Jean Genet, unbuttons his jeans,

watches the thunderheads collide,
while two lovers in a nearby loft
feed their albino pigeons. In Prague

someone puts violets on Kafka's grave.
A student clasps the cello between her knees,
tightens the bow, tunes the A string,

and begins to play, cantabile.
Her downstairs neighbor bangs
with a broom on the ceiling.

Unexpectedly, a sadness surfaces
among all of them; a sheen of sheer light,
as apparent as desire, falls

through all the cracks in the walls,
illuminating for each of them
what is missing, what is always

already gone, beyond
anyone's capacity for grief.

## Costume Drama

*No, do thy worst, blind Cupid,*
*I'll not love.* Lear, IV. vi

The heart has no knowledge of its own recesses
in which dramas are scripted by strangers,
rehearsed, staged, and then cancelled

in the midst of the second act.
There's trash in the aisles of the theatre
and a lonely janitor, drunk to the gills,

whose push broom misses most of it.
The stage sets are chopped up for kindling.
It's thirty below outside. The streets are bare.

In the aftermath of the performance,
when the actors have slunk home, swearing,
the heart gets quietly tight and sings

to itself on the Barcalounger
in bogus foreign accents
about passion, adultery, betrayal.

Yet the heart is undeterred.
Again it sets out to furnish its dramas,
goes to garage sales and second-hand stores,

choosing its soundtracks: Wagner, Puccini,
recorded on scratched vinyl records,
and its costumes— slouched hat, tweed cape,

harlequin's mask, and bulletproof vest.

## The Glass Children

All day the sea has paid them no heed
so they have straggled along the hedgerows,
pining after rabbits and stray fish.

Having been to the opera so often
they are as resonant as glass
and will sleep tonight dreaming

of escalators and esplanades.
Their heads, nestled on pillows of glass,
are so heavy their eyelids shatter,

and the blind can see them blinking
in sepia photographs
under vast, inviolate skies.

## Nursery Rhymes

Dissolute like grass
eyes the color of sleep or his brother

he became himself over and over
while I waited behind the wet wall,

threw a baseball over the mansion, wishing
the sky would come out of hiding.

*Now we are six,* he said, smiling
at the indolent ice-cream vendor,

*and now we are sad.* He jumped.
So I sat at the gate and played my violin

till the moon went down and the cows came in.
Did they tell you

what the beggar said when he bowed his head
and faded away in the rain? He said,

*Now we are sick*
*and then we go mad*

as the winds blow blackly over the sea
and the delicate sailboats drown.

## Valentine's Day

Walking through new snow
and the white light that suffuses the air,

it is not possible to breathe
without inhaling the ascerbic beauty

that etches the eyes and lungs with ice
and deposits an icy residue

into the ventricle and aorta, so that
the entire body begins to chill

and the heart flowers furiously in the face.

It's the body's last defense against the cold,
while mute, baffled, the feelings stare out

through scarves, steam, and auto exhaust
at the shielded eyes of strangers.

Shrouded, people trudge along sidewalks,
carrying bundles and packages

as if there were some imperative for feeling
in this indifferent serenity.

## Sleepwalkers

His paper face, she thought, I'll burn it,
and maybe she did, years later.  We heard
she moved to Brittany, raised their son

who drowned in the spring tides.  Not true.
She bought a condo in Fort Walton,
married, grew camellias.  Still

water followed her, and when his face
exploded, she was listening
to a Hindemith quartet while

polishing pearl-handled knives.

After all that sleep, nothing but more sleep,
and after all those dreams, more stupid dreams:
her lungs like silk, his eyelids crumpled,

they lay down in the dark
the way sleepwalkers move along railings,
touching but not touching.

She's pretending
to know where he's been, though in fact

there's a tear askew in his eye,
and something jagged on his cheek

like an unchecked memory
begins to gather weight.

If he turns away now, their grievances
will proliferate, innumerable windows

that someone closes, one by one,
until the distance goes blind

and they are left standing in the bedroom,
seeing themselves, once again,

absorbed by receding mirrors,
so thin that their flesh begins to settle

into its own gravitational fields:
acres of worn-out sunlight

subterranean in their sleep.

## Toward the End

There is no time for time anymore.
Air surfs toward an unknown destination,
mountains bunch up as if alarmed

and these few leaves that drift
like dislocated alphabets
no longer describe ruptures in feeling.

A gray light rattles the windows. It's as if
all our regrets had blinded us
and sitting aslant from each other

we nod and murmur assent.

The last light peels off the horizon,
layer by layer,
until the heart chooses its statue and stands still.

Disaster always possesses this
perfect geometry,
a symmetrical crossfire of intentions.

Seated around the table,
our hands transparent on our wineglasses
we are on the verge of speech

when the sunlight freezes.

The end is more subtle and remorseless
than we could have ever imagined, watching
the stiff birds shatter in the breeze.

## Fugitives

I.

At midnight someone plays the accordion
in the rue de Polignac. It's too hot for sleep
so we sing to each other, sotto voce,
desolate lullabies.

In Rieka we pawned our watches.
In Dubrovnik we dove from the cliffs.
We traveled to Pec with black-clad peasants
who wailed while the driver gulped Slivovitz,

and surrendered our passports
in that grotty train station in Titograd,
soldiers weeping, chickens
screeching in the bathroom stalls.

Now our eyelashes flap in the dark. Strangers even
to our mirror images,
which pose in the hallways of cheap hotels,
it seems we will always flee our pursuers

causing the dwellers in towns by the tracks
to fall in a dull sleep and dream of our arrival
in some cold, still, empty place,
over the mountains, past

all dread of discovery.

II.

Dubrovnik is past rescue. Its cliffs over the Aegean
recite verses in other languages.
Bleakly beautiful, it floats to the east.

I don't know where I live. I remember everything
but this absence, a hole in my wrist
where the tides wash in. I have been remiss.

Near the railroad station a cat is crying, lonely.
On the Grand'Place a crowd has gathered, dazed with
alcohol and heat. Music breaks from the sky.

We read omens in the flight of birds:
oil spills, the collapse of currencies,
puncture wounds in the atmosphere

beyond which nothing attends to us
but a few lunatics with telescopes in a galaxy
that no longer moves at the speed of light

but is jammed in some corner,
honking its horn, spinning the dial
on the shortwave radio

from which no one speaks.

## Haunted

*Qui suis-je? Si par exception, je m'enrapportais à un adage: en effet pourquoi tout ne reviendrait-il pas à savoir qui je 'hante'?*
—André Breton, *Nadja*

Alone, I think of small ruptures
beginning in the hand, moving
along the shattered secrets of the mouth.

The tree line retreats, mountains describe
small arcs in departing air,
villages fuse with frost and disappear.

*Somewhere it must be snowing*
*past all indifference.*

Thinking of him does no good.
For example, this window, having
shed its delicate crust,

begins to snarl toward detail,
ripple with ragged light like a '30s movie.

I wanted to walk on my head, like Lenz,
but the roads in my eyes were too tired,
and the camera angles collapsed

into one long shot. Fade-out.
Darkness. Slowly the audience
steps outside into new snow

inlaid upon windshields, almost perfect,
the way ghosts remember us when they look down.

## Residue

There is a certain sweetness in winter
which collects upon parapets and skylights
and drips slowly on the snowy earth

like the residue of some half-forgotten moment
last April or May, when two companions
paused for a moment, leaned on the railing,

contemplating the distant city
and the wooded hills folding behind it
and uttered some small, personal truth

perhaps for the first time— a confession,
a fleeting feeling—
before moving on, casually

as if nothing had happened. Now
in winter, distance has become
white and visible all around us,

and the heart itself is chilled, impermeable,
sleepwalking through snowfields
as if they were mined

clad in its stolen furs.

## A Revelation

The bruised gardenia, drunk on its own sweetness,
lies in a bowl of water, listening
to the Ravel Concerto in G, slow movement,

as a patent-leather darkness covers
the French windows, and unexpectedly
a nail clipping of a moon appears.

It's a revelation!

All this time we had believed in time,
in progress, the ballot box, vitamin supplements, and yet

there were black balloons flying at half-mast,
dreams of ineffable sadness,

bungee jumpers bouncing off bridges
while playing the viola da gamba,

and those dark, disconsolate strangers
loitering on street corners
as if transfixed by desire and grief.

In the cerebellum's folds that sweetness lingers,
a time bomb with white petals
to detonate this dull existence

with its sitcoms and shopping carts.
Let us decamp.
The landlord won't pursue us.

Some irate neighbor will have the car towed. Music will spill
like water from a sluice
and we will discover the difference between

money and justice, daylight and knowledge,
suicide and hope.

# III.
# Hyperopia

*'Tis the times' plague, when madmen lead the blind.*
Lear, IV. i

## Daylight

A mild rain in the shadows of the pines:
the air is washed.  Inaudible

like voices from the past,
the wind converses with the clouds.

Vestiges of dreams
disappear: coffee and daylight.

A bulldozer begins its work
of disruption; a leaf blower roars.

Frightened, the gray squirrels scatter.

The *Times* lies upon the doorstep.
Far away, by fiat or disaster,

strangers lie dead in the rubble of cities.

## Revolution

The blue has been with us ever since we left,
all long hair and longing.

In the evenings we leaned over the grand piano,
At midnight we waltzed on the tennis courts.

Everyone we knew looked dangerous and beautiful.
Everything we did seemed perfect

and violent. Now
we are trapped in that blue that is leaving us

at the speed of night, or faster,
so that our faces blur in the mirrors,

the chandeliers crash to the parquet floors,
and the shiny green Bentley, driven

at full speed by our crazed chauffeur, goes
right through the wall and out on the

Champs Élysées. The crowd
cheering. The blade of the guillotine flashing.

We deserve our deaths, such as they are,
theatrical, even tasteless,

to atone for all those times we turned away, saying,
*it's not my fault.*

## May Day

*The goal of the revolution is the abolition of fear.*
—Theodor Adorno

In every rebellion there's an instant
when street corners look like movie sets and
the protestors feel self-conscious, like
extras in *Ben-Hur.* Just now

beyond the barricades, some invisible gesture
has frozen everyone in place—
blue-jacketed workers, defiant students,
the police massed behind their lexite shields.

We could have spent the afternoon like good bourgeois,
lounging on the balcony
sipping Earl Grey, listening to Fauré,
but something cramped inside us

wanted to escape; something smooth
wanted to be scraped raw,
so we dragged our bikes from the cellar,
pedaled toward the Sorbonne, shouting

*la lutte continue*! Flushed

with fear and desire, flayed
ragged by the wind, we were
as vivid as red flags. And now
crouching on the cobblestones,

waiting for the reel to jerk into motion,
hearts drumming, we notice the smallest attributes
of the ordinary world— a faded poster
for Leo Ferré, the smell of car exhaust

mingled with tear gas, and how
trapped in the bistro window,
a black fly crawls, sometimes steadily,
then erupting into furious

motion— seeking
that visible, inaccessible liberty.

# Aesthetics and Politics

*Es ist niemals ein Dokument der Kultur, ohne zugleich ein solches der Barbarei zu sein.*
— Walter Benjamin

In Sarajevo people run screaming
through the marketplace, trampling blood into flowers,

while we sit stunned in Alice Tully Hall,
stupid with delight, listening

to a Mozart piano quartet,
discursive, eloquent, like a conversation

among geniuses: philosopher, poet,
mathematician, painter.

The stone nave of an imaginary cathedral
soars overhead: Canterbury

or Chartres, with its 12th-century windows
the blue of crushed sapphires

and its two spires, one late Gothic
the other older and simpler, *the most perfect*

wrote Henry Adams, *piece of architecture in the world.*

When the music concludes, the pianist pauses,
fingers poised over the keys

as the last note hovers in the balcony,
and at the same instant, a Bosnian child

face blown into anonymity, also
ceases to draw breath. It is

cold in the center of our fists, our chests.
Beauty outlives us.

## The Delicate World

It looms like a landscape in our sleep
but our broken binoculars fail
to establish the boundaries

of the vast yellow field interrupted by windmills.
The delicate world persists
out of eyeshot.  Now

there is such difficulty in sustaining
the breach that has opened
between wind and window, eye and eyelash.

We are sluggish here, confined
to our metal desks, our nightmares
of mortgages and small beer.

We would swell in the wind like spinnakers
if someone would untie us
so that at last we could drift into liquid space,

radical, with blue trees
and red flowers blooming beneath us
to mark our liberation

from the gravity of the past.

## New World Order

I'm an insomniac island, a bruise, an implacable groan.
Gazing out my windows, I figure

that some will expire, others survive, the rest
live in fear of the earthquakes.

Executions are televised daily.
"Each citizen becomes an overseer."

I speak to no one. I have barred my doors.
My bungalow is guarded by alarm systems.

At sunset the Joshua trees flame up. The desert
undulates around me like a dry ocean.

I am a lover of beauty.

Children press their lips on the windows.
*We are homeless and hungry*, they whisper.

I shoo them away.
These are dangerous times; you can't trust anyone.

With my telescope, I make sure they depart.
They are small and brown and mournfully human.

Helicopters and SWAT teams prowl at night,
terrifying the neighbor's dog

who also fears the passing of the past.

## New Age Blues

I.

The astrologer ponders conjunctions of Mars
with Venus, inescapable destinies
transiting the world like a spray of bullets

in search of innocent prey. We're just
looking for love or a televised accident
that everyone miraculously survives,

getting drunk afterwards,
filing fraudulent insurance claims
and celebrating sleeplessness

as if it were a calm subtropical sea.

Then it's the doorbell again,
the salesman an extraterrestrial,
with his wind chime spirituality

promising a world that makes sense,
smells like peppermint, and pays dividends.
How could we have languished so long without him?

II.

Like a mantra seeking to articulate
something banned and baffling,
a comet crumbles in the western glow.

Amateur astronomers weep with joy
at the sight of something dim and distant
circulating to no purpose,

delinquent, like an overdue bill
wrongly addressed and forwarded
to an empty house.  Meanwhile

palmists slouch in their tents, deciphering
hands veiled in failing light
though their angle of vision occludes each glimpse

into what is future or absent.

What the world is and where it is going,
what trajectory desire takes
as it annihilates its objects

how dreams elide the broken pillars
that separate space from time,
none of this is visible

in the crystal ball on the psychic's table,
the refracting lens of the telescope,
or the microscope's scrutiny of dust.

III.

Ours is the half-life of nuclear insomnia.

The stars stagger through silken darkness,
beckoning, perhaps menacing us,
or, most likely, oblivious

to our sufferings— the sky illegible,
empty of gods and alien spaceships,
veiled in its spume of clouds and light,

always abandoning us.

IV.

The eye is a lucid pool of water
into which comets and asteroids fall,

the detritus of galaxies. Space
is a mathematical construct,

calculated by computers, measured
by radio telescopes, riddled with

black holes and parallel universes.
Thus I wait in line at the grocery store

with only five items and am nonetheless
fixed till infinity, learning from

*The National Enquirer* that life is
irrational and unsavory, not

chaste and logical like the stars.

V.

The sky's tyrannical calm
and the storm's dictatorial violence fall

together in tropical latitudes
where we lie with our eyes lashed shut,

our bodies limp in their hammocks.
Sky after sky after sky, we

ponder strategies of resistance.
Eye after eye, we see them

the grid and the crosshairs, moving
over targets that always escape us.

The veins lunge in the wrist.
The heart thuds on the lungs.

Nothing can make the world move.
Not a fist. Not a scream. Not a gunshot.

VI.

If the sky goes blank, there is no one to see it
collapse into itself, gathering cold clouds

and climbing its banisters into another sky,
colder and farther away.

There is this distance, always, in the midst of us,
waiting to return and recover all that we have lost.

There is this silence that no one can hear,
shattering our sleep.

VII.

The bay is flat and still.  Sailboats
float on it, becalmed.

A bridge adheres to the bare horizon.

I rush past on rapid transit
in a glaze of iron and noise, my

newspaper sagging south.  It's not
rational to reflect upon water

reflecting the air, to feel exultant
yet on the verge of tears,

bored yet nearly drowning
in the spill of light from the empty sky,

which does not even know we are here,
goes as far from us as space allows

and is as loud as silence itself.

Like the skull after death,
cold, clanking calcium.

It's that steel we were born with, in our fingers,
vibrating against vacancy,

communicating nothing to no one.

VIII.

Newspapers lie on café tables,
their headlines drooping

with the weight of immense messages.
Letter by letter they devour themselves

until they become trees again.
Weather prediction: cold,

then colder, with a few cirrus clouds
scudding over the foothills,

an outbreak of beauty so poignant
that we are advised to wear dark glasses

to keep our tears in check.

## Happenstance

As indifferent as plutocrats,
stars roll down their bowling alleys,

earthquakes shatter adobe houses,
copycat killers pursue lone women

down the backstreets of Yorkshire towns.

The randomicity reckoned in statistics
adds up to this:

the right place at the wrong time.
The glass vase topples from a windowsill,

kills a passer-by. A sunburn

triggers melanoma. Drunk
drivers speed down narrow streets.

A bomb in the métro will murder
all those who, by happenstance,

headed for the Isle St.-Louis
for Bertillon ice cream,

her winsomeness, his quirks,
their crooked smiles— abolished.

Accountants will calculate their absence,
the loss of productivity, the cost of training

people to replace them.

## Armistice Day

I.

No one in November goes anywhere.
We look as remote as the sky that

foamed over us and exploded. At noon
old soldiers on parade floats chant their

names, ranks, & serial numbers.

Sometimes I feel like God in an envelope.
The blood is invisible but

you can smell it beneath the gray headstones.
Vast and incessant the violence continues.

II.

When we woke up, everything resumed—

new recruits shouting in the Champs de Mars,
legless men selling hot chestnuts,

a spotted plover on frozen wings,
singing reproachfully. You can never

get what you need here.

You can't find a shriek on the sidewalk
or a dime in the air.

There is always a messenger running past
and a man on the street corner, screaming.

## Delirium

As Golden Gate Park lies sunken in seafog
concealing in heaps of sodden brown leaves
beer cans, condoms, a soccer ball,

gaunt men clad in denim and leather
stroll through the Castro, hands in their pockets,
past mannequins posed like soldiers.

The earth repeats what the sky has forgotten.
Implacable now, burned landscapes mime
the urban world's slow delirium.

The men line up in hospital corridors,
their black-gloved hands
clasped, bound together for solitary spaces.

Once their bodies were ripe and muscled.
They grappled & coupled,
dark kisses against deep walls.  Now

the stench of ammonia,
the interminable rattle of rain,
the indifference of governments.

## Narcolepsy

*Look, there is the sky and here is the grass.*
— Melville

I.

The sky flashes past us while we sleep,
deep in our beds, drowning,

cello-shaped in our linen sheets,
hands like petals on the pillows.

This morning we were ablaze,
breathing the foul light that streamed

through skyscrapers and subways,
jangling the coins in our pockets.

Someday I'd like to wake up forever from

the dreams I abjure,
toss on my railroad trestle, fall

past all recovery
into millions of loose stars, like dimes

freed from profit and exchange.

II.

He was perplexed by all financial transactions,
could not recall his ATM number,

and arrived at the airport without his luggage
but left anyway— and never returned.

We remember him on Fridays, at the corner,
watching the kids play ball and whistling

*Alle Menschen werden Brüder.*

"You're all expendable," our boss tells us
when he catches us staring out the window

at the Goodyear blimp, or tracing
the Cape of Good Hope with a dazed finger.

And we are. I have been dead
since I first sat down in my cubicle, staring

at this screen in which I could not
see my face.

III.

*I know where I am.*
I could have lived in the suburbs

and read bestsellers, but instead
I play fugues on the glass harmonica in the subway

while accountants and receptionists
rush past me, their ticket stubs

tucked behind their ears.
I feel like flotsam on a beach, detritus.

The dead hold out their hands, imploring,
but impatient we brush past them.

We have nothing more to say to them,
except in our sleep; they are just

tourists waiting at a bus stop
when the drivers are on strike.

Then those postcards arrive
from born-again boroughs, threatening

that the world will end any minute.
*If only it would.*

## Xenophilia

I was like you, once.

In fact, I was you. Now
as the air departs daily from
métro stations and dinosaur exhibits,

it's no longer easy to distinguish
between etiquette and *Angst.*
For example, the gentleman on the bench just

south of me has opened a book and
fallen through a reverie so deep
even death would not disturb it. And the

woman strolling woefully past
has furled her silk umbrella
for the last time. And we are all

wholly and specifically lost.
By the time anyone sees this,
it will be August, cyclists crouching

on their way to the sea. Downstairs
a cellist plays Boccherini
as if he were underwater. Snow

geese form a pattern that
shatters when I pull down the shades,
and I'm in an aquarium:

extinct fish swimming toward land, keening
to themselves, homesick
for another world.